THE DISTAL POINT

THE DISTAL POINT

Fiona Moore

HAPPENSTANCE

BY THE SAME AUTHOR:

Night Letter (pamphlet), HappenStance, 2015
The Only Reason for Time (pamphlet), HappenStance, 2013

ACKNOWLEDGEMENTS:

Thanks to the editors of the following magazines and anthologies
in which poems have appeared: *Brittle Star, Diversifly Anthology,
Emma Press Anthology of Mildly Erotic Verse, London Grip, Magma,
Morley College Anthology, Mslexia, New Boots & Pantisocracies, New
Walk, Orbis, Poems in Which, Poetry London, Smiths Knoll, South Bank
Poetry, Stand, Tears in the Fence, The Compass Magazine, The Bow-Wow
Shop, The Frogmore Papers, The Interpreter's House, The Poetry Review,
The Rialto, The Scotsman, The SHOp,* and *Under the Radar.* 'Seizure'
won second prize in the Poetry & Psychoanalysis competition, 2017.
Some poems also previously appeared in *Night Letter* (HappenStance,
2015) and *The Only Reason for Time* (HappenStance, 2013).

Many thanks also to all my poetry friends and teachers for their
help and support, and in particular to those who commented on
the draft manuscript.

NOTE FOR VISUALLY IMPAIRED READERS:

The book jacket is pale grey with the author's name (italics, lower
case) and the title (caps) in dark green, placed on a band of paler
grey just below the middle of the book. Between the author's name
and the title there is a tiny plane leaf, also dark green.

First published in 2018 by HappenStance Press
21 Hatton Green, Glenrothes KY7 4SD
www.happenstancepress.com

ISBN: 978-1-910131-44-2

Printed and bound by Imprint Digital, Exeter
https://digital.imprint.co.uk

CONTENTS

III   THE ROSE, THE STARS

—I—

OVERWINTER

THE SHIRT

I didn't find it for months, your shirt
bundled into a corner of the airing cupboard.
I shook it out. It had been cut
with long cuts all the way up the sleeves
and up the front, so it looked like a plan
of something about to be put together.
They must have had to work so fast to
save you there was no time to unbutton it.
An office shirt, because that's where
it happened. The thin stripes slashed through—
terrifying, unprecedented—a reminder
of everything I wanted to forget.
I'd washed it afterwards, not knowing what to do
with it, or that in three weeks the same thing
would happen to another shirt, a favourite,
dull cotton whose thick weave made it look
as if all the pink shell-grains of sand
had come together on one beach,
a shirt for a gentle hug; and from then on
nothing happened that we would forget.

ISLAND

The ocean is a garment loosening
and tightening around an uneven neckline:
the sponge of a salt-marsh, the abrupt
drop of a cliff, a beach strewn with flotsam.

At night, whatever the tide, the waves reach
inward through every inlet and river
and transmit a pulse to mark our silence.

By day we are all one ear above the coastline
and the sea is our immersive sound
multiplied differently on every shore.
Ear becomes anvil when the breakers heighten.

Often we seem to be moving with the water
or against. Sun or clouds won't tell us and the stars
are too far off, and on too great a scale.

Even the most violent winter storm
—when for days we breathe the sticky tang of spume
blown here, to the end of the wind's long fetch—
holds a sense of coming resolution;

and even in calm there's the grain-
by-grain pulling away to tell of a change
that's slow, and slow, and one day total.

ON DUNWICH BEACH

The brown sea raids the shore, where you lie not far
inland. I crouch on wet shingle, undressing for you.

I plunge in, slipping where the ground falls away,
gasping at the icy cold: now I'm swimming for you

though you'd never have swum in this, and I know it,
but raise my head with the swell, searching for you.

Waves rock the pale horizon. I could swim on
until my heart falters and I'm dying for you

but I'd never find you. The water's embrace jolts,
heaves, lulls me … I kick hard, breathing for you

through strands of hair … The drab land calls, the sea
spits me out—numb, dripping salt, living for you.

IN LATE NOVEMBER

Time stopped, a crevasse opened at your feet
and you fell headlong. I found you climbing
upward against gravity, masked, learning
to breathe. Drips snaked your limbs, and your shoulder

twisting from the sheet was pale as marble.
When you tried to break through, I called your name,
called you back from somewhere I'd never been,
back to astonishment in a cold factory.

This happened to you in the wrong season.
The last leaves have been downed by wind and rain.
It's dark and no traces survive of growth
or green or blue to float the dread away.

'THE ONLY REASON FOR TIME IS SO THAT
EVERYTHING DOESN'T HAPPEN AT ONCE'
—*Albert Einstein*

I will get language where I can,
I will recover you from time that is not
linear as it seemed. You went out
through its door and will come back in
before you left, and intact.
What could be more ordinary
than this, or easier to say?
You, wearing clothes I've kept,
the Aran jersey of our first kiss, folded
to two dimensions, collapsing time
from its fourth: time, our sealant
in the parallel, never-to-meet
where I live, you rot and your jersey
holds me loosely, warm, undyed.

TOWER

You'd never climb those worn stone
spirals up the tower of a church
or castle. You used to say
it was your bungalow childhood
and your dad making you
climb the Glenfinnan Monument
black and vertiginous inside.
You hated the old staircase
in the hotel at Wirksworth
that swung unsupported
round the edge of a deep well
across which our laughter echoed
while I went up by the slender
iron banisters and you
almost clung to the wall.
As for the towers, I climbed up
on my own. Sometimes
you'd go off to do something else;
other times you'd wait for me
to wave at you from the top.
Once in France a church tower was so
high and you so far away
in the square under plane trees
standing among wavy green
shadows not of water but some
unknown element that I
was afraid of losing you
until I climbed down, found you
and gave you a kiss
to prove myself wrong.

SEIZURE

If your mind at night was a citadel asleep,
safe in its round of bone, while your body did the work
of outer defence, encabled with nerves and blood,
the heartbeat and the breath saying all was well,
then those nights afterwards when I lay next to you,
your long limbs trembling, jerking as you slept,
the citadel had been bombed to near destruction.

Rubble woman helpless, hopeless at the scale of it
I was among ruins not knowing where, the streets
unrecognisable, each outline jagged and smouldering,
and beyond them the stars, too, sparked out of order,
their pathways disrupted, all geometry lost.
To hold you through those long nights was like holding
earth and heaven confused and scattered in my arms.

THE ONCOLOGIST

Poets are meant to suffer. Use it, he said,
sprawled across your bed writing up his notes.
You'd gone out for a pee, the ward was quiet.
I told him how frightening it was, and his look
told me he understood—he'd nursed his wife
and watched death take many of the pale figures
queueing at his clinic.
                    I could see how
he comforted them, as he did us—that look,
the holding of our hands, his blunt, local words
and his keeping alive our hope. *Wasn't hope
the last thing that came out of the box?* he said
to us, who still possessed what he had lost.

Whatever he might say, he was saying
this happens to us all.
                   Once I heard
myself in the voice of a grey-haired woman
who said to him, *Goodbye. You take care, now*—
words full of her own longing that one day
he should be all right, and I understood
how it helped to want to comfort him back,
even though we couldn't.

1010101010...

Your death works in binary mode
on/off, forget/remember—
a cold code to decipher,
too late for us.

Your death kills me a thousand times.
The tyranny of repetition—
you/me, here/there.
Zero/one.

HUNGER

One way to dispose of a corpse is to eat it.

The skeleton lies on my plate, fish-perfect, scavenger food. It reminds me of the last time we ate mackerel together.

Necrophagy. Even the dictionary half-shuns the word. Somewhere between perversion and religion there must be a space for this confusion of eating and death.

After your funeral I was hungry, for the first time in weeks. Beer, sandwiches, tea and cake: death's nursery food. That was months ago. Now I'm full of mackerel, the complete feeling that comes from eating a whole creature.

Necrophagy. Even the dictionary half-shuns the word. Somewhere between perversion and religion there must be a space for this confusion of eating and death.

The skeleton lies on my plate, fish-perfect, scavenger food. It reminds me of the last time we ate mackerel together.

One way to dispose of a corpse is to eat it.

OVERWINTER

This is midwinter's longest day
that absorbs its own silence of waiting.
Nothing moves through the air
and gravity seems a miracle, the earth's grip
made of so much more than frost.
Instead the ground-mist floats the trees
whose outlines are all gesture,
each miming the wait differently.
Nothing will happen for a while, nothing—
and I need such certainty: to become
embedded deep within this season
when dark overplaits the day's pale strand.
Change may come while nothing seems to change.
I know it will take a long time.

THE EMBRACE

It's half dark
and we're lying down
        we embrace, we fade away.
The comfort of it and closeness
but it feels like
        dream.

So different from that time
you walked into the bedroom.
It was early, I
was getting ready to go out and you,
you'd just come back
        from abroad, been
away for weeks and we hugged and hugged.

The jersey you were wearing was
        greenish
unfamiliar. We hugged and
life began to run again through my veins and bones
heart and head, all
the chemicals of awakening
        in one rush.

We wanted to lie down together
but there was no time
so we agreed to meet
later.
        An ordinary conversation
and then the fade.
        Then

the waking.
      You'd been dead
for two and a half months.

It's never happened again
like that, clear as day; and rarely at all
      as if in dreams
what's wanted most becomes what can't be had.

This time the strange thing is
      having reached you
I feel you're at once
both nearer and further away.

GETTING UP AT SIX

Your feet step down each stair
and then, as I hear you gather one by one
the things you heaped on the table late last night

I wonder: what does it feel like to be you
as you stand there filling the small room,
your long reach as you pocket the clatter of change

your knuckles grazing the smooth lining, still cool;
to be you as you slide the lozenge phone into your jacket
as your hand engulfs the thistlehead of keys

(what are they all for?) the wallet, the rail-pass
and you straighten your spine, your shoulders ...

The gate screeches as you lift the cold bar of the latch
and I wonder, half asleep in the circle
of your warmth, what does it feel like to be you ...

As you lope off to the station,
phone bumping against your chest,
what do your hands remember?

UNKNOWN

She'd have been eight now, that lovely age
when the mind, still deep in childhood,
starts to reach out beyond it.
The age you were when your father died.
I picture her with the red hair
of both grandmothers.

Why a girl, I don't know.
A boy might have reminded me better—
that photo of you on your parents' lawn.
Strange to think, after so much, how young
she'd still be, how this would mark
the slowness of years.

Would she have carried
an early memory of you, maybe one
like mine of our last embrace when you
could still stand up, with the bed
behind you for safety?

If you're a ghost that walks
beside me, she is doubly so. But she
grows older with time
whereas you don't—soon
the gap between you and me will show.

OUTSIDE GRAMSCI'S HOUSE

The two of us, smiling at the learned young curator
who'd offered to take our picture. Behind us is the sign
House of Antonio Gramsci and the front door open
into a dark interior. Our shoulders are touching,
we are layered against the cold and you're holding a package,
your hero on a red t-shirt. A vein ridges your hand.

One glance and I'm with you standing on the wet pavement
full of a shared hour spent looking and reading—
his hard life, long imprisonment and early death—
and our journey to get there, steep angled terraces
blazing black and green under white sun, the almond blossom
luminous.
              I didn't keep the t-shirt
but now I see it in your hand, I wish I had.

NIGHT LETTER

I don't believe in an afterlife
any more than you did,
but sometimes at night I lie awake
and can't not imagine you
floating, out there
somewhere between angel and ectoplasm,
because sometimes this is easier
not only for the heart
but for the mind too.

It feels almost disloyal
to you, who said again
there was nothing
after we'd been given the prognosis;
said it calmly, factually. So
if you're out there, please
forgive me for imagining
you, out there.

POSTCARD

Three days and already I could write
a dissertation on the fastenings of gates:

the counterintuitive, industry standard
grey metal latch, to be clanged backwards;

the bolt with a spring that's always too strong;
the soft warmth of an old chain, brown stream

through fingers, binding the post with a hook;
the double gate's hard-edged central loop

with its guillotine rise/drop; and the frayed
Gordian knot of orange nylon twine, avoided

by climbing at the hinge end. Each one
a puzzle, each to be handled and worked on,

each gate lifted or pulled before I pass
from the last room of sheep or meadow flowers—

below hills that move up and down and up
as if walking their own walk—to the next. With love.

AFTER FIVE YEARS

You'll carry in strange dust on your feet
if you come back now: from as far away
as this thought, out of the first twilight
long enough to feel like spring.

Orbiter of legend and distant stars,

here you'll be: dazed by the earth, its green
perfection of circumstance,
the multiplicity of events and things,
what's new and what's stayed the same—

your feet winged by that strange dust.

THE DISTAL POINT

We stand at the point of greatest change—
the distal point, a shingle spit
at the end of the longshore drift.
Here the waves curve
and spill, lacing each other,
forming a landscape that moves
leached of colour.

No-one who stands here
can see down the length
of the wind's fetch
and only the gulls measure
the shape of the swell
as they swing high
on the full, low in the swale

and no-one has stood here before
where each accretion of ground
becomes an erosion
from the diagonal swash
and straight backwash,
the waves' refraction and landfall.
No-one will stand here again.

—II—

EXCLAVE

NUMBERLESS

Sometimes in one of those dreams
where everything is out of place
but only a little, the dreaming self
realises: oh, it was always
that way. The television did
always sit on the narrow work top,
bulging slightly. You always had
a green Paisley scarf that you'd knot
at your pyjama neck, someone
out of Brideshead. With a small
jolt of surprise and acceptance
last night I realised that a colleague
had waited forever down the road
in his car for me to direct him
through Greenwich, past the convent
skyscraper (30's Chicago style,
purple granite), and say *mind the nun
and the other women,* one of whom
(his vestments covered with crosses)
was a priest and my dream-self
found it right to refer to him thus.
The colleague had always had
a snowstorm of stubble, which thickened
during the journey. It's as if
the dream were acknowledging
numberless permutations
of daily life so our waking selves
don't need to, otherwise long ago
I'd have walked through the upstairs
bedroom window which leads,
by now, to many places.

1985

Another cold day, another visit. He could be a provincial governor or in charge of a sector of heavy industry. Or someone with a senior party post, maybe even a secretary of the central committee. None of these admits foreigners often or willingly, at least not westerners.

The usual shoddy office, higher-ceilinged than most, a large wooden desk and beige plastic upholstery on the seventies easy chairs. Today though, something stands out. One of the phones is red. Scarlet: a clenched fist on the desk between him and us. What's it been used for? To order arrests, discuss calling the army out against the workers, say it's ok to shoot? He'd be told, of course, he wouldn't do the telling. But he'd have a voice and he'd be passing things on. What questions do you ask a man like this?

The telephone wires are all in a tangle off the front of the desk. The red phone may have an old-fashioned circular dial or push-buttons; both models are possible.

EXCLAVE

Place that's always seen as over the horizon,
that exists outside the boundary of what defines it.
Ghost ship apart from the fleet or ice calf from berg,
goose away from the skein. Jigsaw of a cottage,
half a window lost between floorboards or hoovered up
long ago with the dust. A memory of someone
still held in the mind, though it feels more like the heart.
My absence, anyone's absence from the crowd.
Outland, outlandish. It takes the longest time
to get there, and the longest time to leave.

We drove to the frontier once, or as far as we could:
unmetalled road through ragged fields and birch,
the only oddness the lack of houses or people.
We came to a log on posts that blocked our way
and nailed on the log was an ordinary road sign,
a blank white circle outlined in red. We looked
into silence: the trees and fields empty of
barbed wire, a mine strip, high guard towers
with a gate, if any, only to be opened
at the end of the world as we knew it.

THE NUMBERS

The numbers. Etched in faded indigo: maybe half a dozen, small and precise.
On close inspection, blurred as if the skin had puckered them
rather than they the skin. The lower arm's soft skin, another vein
                                        or blotch of age.

Occasionally—
just as you might board the same tram as usual but arrive
                                        somewhere unexpected—
occasionally it would happen. In random settings and conversations
someone would push up a sleeve and show me the numbers. Always casually
and as a matter of fact.

TAKING VISITORS TO AUSCHWITZ

It's here
except it's not.
This could be anywhere or on the edges of.
That car's parked askew
and sparrows forage on the tarmac
while people pose each other at the entrance.

This is not a place to visit twice:
better to stay outside
and pick them up again.

Coaches drop off groups.
A dull day, no snow or frost:
winter it is or on the edges of,
bare poplars line a field beyond the wire
here in the ordinary carpark.

Better to wait,
better to wait
here, in the ordinary carpark.
Bare poplars line a field beyond the wire.
Winter it is or on the edges of,
a dull day no snow or frost.

Coaches drop off groups
and pick them up again.

Better to stay outside—
this is not a place to visit twice—
while people pose each other at the entrance

and sparrows forage on the tarmac.
That car's parked askew.
This could be anywhere or on the edges of

except it's not,
it's here.

PALACE OF CULTURE

Access is forbidden, like most things
in the realm of the angel of death.

From below, outside, it's a funeral cake
viewed in a distorting mirror.
Inside, the only angel is death

as you rise through layer after layer
built for the greater glory of placemen.
Such a pretty place to fall from
in the realm of the angel of death.

Lift doors open onto air. You could ride
the city's rebuilt roofs like waves.
Concrete pinnacles make you tender
towards cathedrals for being so mocked
but up here the only angel is death

and your mind makes good a lack of signs
for danger. The lifts are original.
A bell pings, doors open onto
darkness forty-two floors deep.
Your descent is a journey like any other
in the realm of the angel of death.

EDEN

(by the river Narew, near Różan, north-east Poland, 1986)

Where nature spewed out immaculate crowds
of baby frogs in a chemical reaction,
grass-green, brown, leaping all over the meadow.

Where each butterfly was new as an invention,
each beetle an exact blueprint, and damselflies
swarmed in storm-clouds above the tangled riverbank

and night was the colour of the damselflies,
starlit perfection, the frogs' echo chamber,
then a swish of rain and the warm smell of earth.

Where storks balanced the messy bar of their nests
on telegraph poles and barn roofs, and the sun
swung higher each day, as if it would forever.

Where all the horizons were limitlessly flat,
stands of pine forest alternating with rye—
then the rye field I walked into one day, led by a path

of trodden stalks, to the secret square brimming
with opium poppies, white/purple bleed of petals,
seed pods about to swell, the shock of intention.

MUSEUM

The walls of the museum are papered with lies.
Each lie lasts as long as the lights stay on
and the lights go out when we leave each room.

All the rooms have wood parquet flooring,
floors polished by felt-slippered feet,
six sliding feet, our own and the guard's—

guard because this feels like a prison.
People go to prison for jokes in this country
so they joke by grinning and shaking their heads

at the giant head on hoardings: the President.
In here, President and Madame smile in photo
after photo, welcoming delegations:

here he welcomes peasants in national dress
singing national songs who offer him fruit
yet fruit and vegetables are unknown to the shops,

the bare-shelved shops. Just noodles and cans,
canned fish pyramids in window displays.
This display's The Flowering of Industry:

flowers for Madame from car plant workers
but the cars they make are not on the streets,
streets that are empty at night, and dark

as the dark of the museum's windowless walls.
One wall in each room is painted red
with the reddest red in the last, empty room.

POLITICAL CABARET, DRESDEN

Everyone in the theatre was the man on the park bench
in a beige mac under an old-style lamp half-lit for dusk.

The detail of the park could never be British, something about
the exactitude of small railings bordering the grass.

He started to talk to a younger man in a leather jacket
leaning against the lamp-post. Their everyday conversation

spanned half a century of years which should not have had
to happen, and somehow they were both to blame and both victims—

everyone in the theatre was the man on the park bench
and everyone was the leather-jacketed secret policeman.

THE CELL AT PLÖTZENSEE

Hitler the vegetarian had the conspirators
hanged from meathooks. A photo survives: pale bodies
in a row, hanging. Unless only the hooks are shown

and I've drawn the bodies from a slaughterhouse image
of carcasses in fat and flesh, or human corpses—Belsen,
chemical weapon victims, the naked hells of Bosch.

The stench at one end of a foreign meat market
once made me nearly throw up. I have never knowingly
smelt the smell of the dead but years ago I worked

in a small palace in Warsaw whose basement had been used,
it was said, as a prison by the Gestapo:
a damp corridor lined with cells of blackened brick

where crates of beer and Coke were stacked, and cardboard boxes
of tinned mince and stew. I had to go down there at night
for security checks but never truly sensed a ghost

nor, upstairs, did I ever see the pale-gowned lady
who was supposed to walk the ballroom floor's scarred wood,
only my own reflection in the tall windows.

The Führer's order was for them to be hanged like cattle.
Hanging from hooks was meant to last longer. Their deaths
may have been filmed, though no film survives unless in some

hidden cabinet of secrets or dark net. The meat-hooks
could be slid along the flange of the high iron beam
where five still dangle in a line, narrow and bare.

QUAKE

The dark never changes, the dark stays dark,
the same things come out of it that always came:
 nothing + nothing is an answer.
The O of the eye, the sun, the ocean, stopped
by doors and ceilings and windows of earth:
 nothing + nothing is an answer.
The bejewelled din, heart of the storm,
an arm in a sleeve, a face clothed in blood:
red is old and a city like silence,
 nothing + nothing is an answer.
Night floods the day as water the sky,
the O of the cave, the whirlpool, the wormhole:
nothing + nothing is nothing, is all,
 nothing + nothing is an answer.

We started debating the flavours of Wall's
Neapolitan—strawberry, then vanilla
and either chocolate or pistachio,
depending on whether or not they stand for
the Italian flag. Not that my childhood
memories are about its taste but rather
a cold creaminess, generically sweet—
the flavours were just a descant, an extra
joy floating above the rest and a choice
of which one to quarry out first. Something
magical lurked in the block: the boundaries
between stripes weren't visible like a drawn line
but a concept arising at the end of, say,
green, and the start of white. How did they
make the bands stick together so neatly,
without blurring? Part of the pleasure of
eating was that it went with this thought,
never voiced. Would anyone still know
how to do that? To find out, you might search
in a factory archive: rust-stained filing
cabinets stuffed with typewritten pages
of industrial secrets. But the factory
has probably long closed and you'd have to
visit some gleamingly international
HQ which would refuse to allow you in.
At last you'd find the retired supervisor,
now proud of the stripes on his front lawn,
who'd explain the recipe and show you
photos of the production line before
they sold it for scrap. Whatever the process
and flag or none, it's impossible not

to keep reverting to the state of things—
for example that parties of the right
would split over what the third colour should be
and how high the walls, though all would agree
the world's not melting. So how was it done—
an invisible, taste-and-textureless
ingredient glueing each join, or a certain
property infusing the whole? Or they dropped
each frozen strip into place and pressed them
lightly together. It could be that simple.

THE RACE

Bullocks—
by this fence
sheltering under the trees,
a paint chart of browns—
startled, they look up, jostle
and they're away!
Down the hill, the green straight
at a gallop—
all bunched up
shouldering each other,
muddy rumps rocking
up/down, hooves
thundering, rope-tails
flying … oh, the rain
roars for them
and the trees too—
the dark one has it
by a head from the roan
and the skewbald—
they're making such time
until they all loosen,
slow, fan out, gentle
themselves into a walk
as if they know exactly
when they've passed
their finishing line.

LOUKANIKOS

The demo's on, the chant's begun and look, it's Loukanikos.
In no man's land between riot squad and crowd sits
                                        Loukanikos.
Bottles and stones may clash with clubs and shields
in the heat of Greek battle, but nothing ever hits
                                        Loukanikos,
ur-dog to our ur-selves, yellowish, middle-sized,
wolf nose and ears that launched a thousand e-fits,
                                        Loukanikos
named for the sausage he loves. He stands four-square
with his masked anarchist gang, braced to dodge the blitz,
                                        Loukanikos
behind the municipal bins, then weaves through legs
and smoke, his tail curled high, unscathed: no-one outwits
                                        Loukanikos.
When all turns quiet he lopes down shattered streets
to the Hotel Grande Bretagne. Though he enjoys the glitz,
                                        Loukanikos
continues the struggle there, lying around and
tripping up foreign bankers and their deficits.
                                        Loukanikos—
dog who adores a riot, political dog,
Diogenes of the front line, dog who never quits—
                                        Loukanikos!

SINK DRAIN

As much a place
as a thing—a space,
or rather a star
in space, iron star,
utilitarian
mid-20th-century
war decoration.
Six discoloured spokes
wheeling outwards
from a hollow circle
and ringed by stainless steel.

As much a symbol
as a place. The Order
of the Kitchen Sink:
for years of hard labour spent
digging out potato peel
and grains of left-over rice,
bent over the black hole
where we'll all end—space,
gut hole, wormhole,
place or non-place.

TIMETABLE

The timetables are striped to help you read them.
There is no meaning to the stripes.

The stripes are pale so you only see them
subconsciously: your brain makes columns

of the numbers which you read as a timetable
because they are in the accepted format—

a list of place-names down the left-hand side,
symbols at the top and very little on a Sunday—

posted on a station wall at the back of beyond.
Otherwise they could be share prices, pace charts,

experimental data or the jottings
of an obsessive. The railway tracks curve

past overgrown embankments, late summer
standstill. You are the only person here.

Some things unravel through explanation.
How did you get this far?

THE COWS OF NORTH KOREA AND SATELLITE SHINING STAR-1

We are the cows who do not exist
except in your mind. We orbit the Earth
on satellite Kwangmyongsong-1,
whose launch, they say, was a national success
just like the production of milk, though we

do not exist. Except in the mind
of the official who zoomed us up to orbit
forever, circling the world, chewing the cud
from the grass on Kwangmyongsong-1 ...
All because of some foreigner asking:

If this is the main dairy region
and rumours of famine are lies, where
are the cows? He answered: The cows
were all sent up with Kwangmyongsong-1
which is, let me tell you, a national success.

So now we're in orbit, grazing the grass
of Kwangmyongsong-1, turning the world ...
Look up at night and you may see our eyes
flash. Remember us. One day you
could become space debris too.

—III—

THE ROSE, THE STARS

THIS VERY ROOM

It will happen soon—the man will appear
in the room where he has been
for a long time in my thoughts.
A particular moment will deliver him
which is what time sometimes does: a ghost
of the imagination so habituated
that his appearance might be caused by
longing rather than by the real man,
flesh and blood as he is, having travelled here
by train and walked up the hill.
Flesh and blood—not that he's those to me
beyond the loving, momentary embrace.
I can see him displace invisibility,
reading along my bookshelves
or in profile looking out the window at the trees,
interested as he always is, but this time
here. He'll enjoy the poster of Polish cartoons
and I'll tell him their story,
how the censors refused permission for the one
of the sea and a post on which hangs
a lifebelt entwined with barbed wire.
How I forget that it's not there.

'O THAT INSISTENT THOUGHT...'

—George Seferis

The river's surface had many variables:
downstream flow, tides, weather and unknown.
　　Our house reflected it on white ceilings, to be read
like the palm of a hand whose fortune kept changing.
　　Stacked up against a cardboard factory
the narrow rooms held a riverine smell, and old
　　sounds: ripples slapping on wooden piles,
and machinery next door, recycling.

One night a mouse ran and ran in the attic
until we trapped her under a cardboard box
　　and left her on the quay in the dark, to act out
the mind that concentrates on one thing and
　　gnaws at it, eating its own page into lace.
By dawn the box had a hole, facing deep
　　water as the mouse would have—stopped
on the edge of something immense.

POEM IN WHICH I THINK MYSELF OUT

Bare foot stepping on a bumble bee's shadow:
it ought to sting. Too many
pink roses for one bee. How far can a pair
of socks be hurled
if the tops are rolled round each other.
People might think
the pink retro sports car outside
belongs to me. Laura Robson's tennis skirt
is made from a bed valance:
go Laura, but not
into the world of unnecessary soft furnishings
or that sort of car—
vandal target, metallic powder puff.
Strange how powder blue and pink exist,
but powder green
is unthinkable. My mother's glass powder jar
and her seated at the three-sided
dressing-table mirror, my face
white at its corners.
On the tube, long rows of heads
repeated through the glass
of each connecting door. Do I
exist when I'm not in the mirror;
and what if
the large rusty manhole
on the swimming-pool floor
were to open. Our bodies
jammed in the sewer like pale fish.

DARK CAR

It does not carry the burden of its mistake.
The effect is of floating, as if without lights
there is no possibility of sound
or because it's coasting, slowly, on the empty road, waiting for green
so it can accelerate away
through the portal.
The car is a silvery saloon, company car.
What it passes moves along its body, reflected,
a camouflage of little gleams.
Inside the car is someone's internal landscape, with flaws,
some conjunction of which has led to the mistake.
It's dark here:
the driver must find it dark between the streetlamps' orange pools
too far apart on the wet road.
Locked in his own armour, unaware of what anyone else would see.
Or fail to see.
I don't try to look inside, though without headlights it should be easy.
I do almost wave, not that he'd notice my kerbside form
but something stops me—
maybe I don't want to become complicit in the mistake
by acknowledging it.
The car is a rarity,
a death foreseen aslant, the night coach slowing for a lonely junction,
horses and coachman headless.
It accelerates smoothly,
passes by.
Without rear lights it is lost under the railway bridge
in shadow and strip lighting.

BURIAL GROUND

This is how gods view the earth, or how one mortal
gazes at another who is naked—lush, road-scarred,

flawed by dry patches, rippled with fat-folds and wrinkles
and silvery rivulets of desire. Today this earth

is pocked and marked by graves: piled-up mounds of the new,
sunken hollows of the old, tabs in rows like a plant nursery

little, oh little. Tumuli of the ancient and whole cities
squashed close, our marble shanty-towns—necropolis,

mausoleum, sepulchre, vault ... No such ceremony
in forest or desert, unmarked sites visible if at all

only from above, that may or may not ever be
exhumed. Or in the field-patch of an island graveyard,

a plot just out of the sea's reach to be rocked, rocked
forever by the waves. All this because yesterday

I visited yours. The higher I go, the fewer
burials can be seen, the more imagined from where I sit

in the middle of life, necessarily blind to anything
beyond the walls and the window's nearest horizon.

INTERRUPTION

Crrrrr crrrrr crrrrr crrrrr
is a crow ringing is a
telephone hopping blackly across the grass
and you're in my ear saying
is my memory a burden to you?
your voice
matter-of-fact but also concerned.
No
this never occurred to me until you
asked (who asked?). It's a fine thing
to live with though I'd rather
live with you. Look over there
on a bench—woman & man
making what they can of each other
and here I am hearing voices
when I'd only expected
to get across the park as fast as possible
through the trees now gone
into their mode of winter,
their growth away slow from their sapling selves
but the shape still visible in them.

RANNOCH MOOR

Any bird up here
       is interesting, small up-
flight out of lunar ground
       sown green and pockmarked
with bog and shiny lochans
       where everything stretches for
miles as the sun sets
       white and the moor lifts
over mountains.

       It would be possible
to get off here or
       here, at these unassuming
stations, to acknowledge
       the strung-out ceremony
of their names
       that mark a tilt southwards,
an irretrievable
       loosening of rhythm
as the train runs
       down the map.

SINGING BIRD

Up somewhere in the foreshortened
row of plane trees, high in their crowns
and singing on a feedback loop—
whee oo whee oo, then a carousel
of other notes—the bird sets off
an echo of myself that I can't find.
The sky's a locked-in grey, the air
overwarm and the bird in December
singing not my heart out but
an element impartial, indifferent
which I'm not—the islands within me
are sinking and I'm afraid
that this bird so loud and clear
may be a blow-in unable to
survive in the park or that the song,
not song thrush not blackbird, *whee
oo whee,* in this time of changes
all the greater for being invisible,
is itself undergoing a change.
I could divert under the seedball
pendulums but fear impels me
forward: I leave the song behind.

CITY FROM A HILL, THROUGH OPEN WINDOWS

Listen to the silence
of eight million sleeping—curled, sprawled,
together or alone—
a counterpane of bodies, each
held in its own breath-filled cell. Not all
asleep. Each sleep
interlocks with the next: is this
what the dawn reveller shouts out against?

Our dreams are
London's underworld, our murmurs form
the backing for one wren
that crowns itself and the dawn with a song
repeated, repeated: echoed
distantly by another.

THE SOUND CROWDS MAKE

The tube bursts out of its tunnel
into the wider cylinder of the station. People filter
from tube to platform, platform to tube. The doors

slam: but one set has trapped
a boy—his neck clamped in the rubberised edges,
double guillotine, and the nearby crowd says

oh, a collective moan of shock.
He's about ten, stuck, head inside the train, body
outside, between two worlds, snagging both of them.

The doors relax—not enough—and thud
closed again with what seems, against his neck, brutal force
as more people say OH, with protest in it this time

and some try to pull the doors
apart, but it happens again and a huge OH! goes up
and shouts pass down the platform to the driver's end.

The boy stays still, silent. OH!
fourth time—disbelief—then the doors open. He stumbles
backwards into people's arms, his face red and blank.

The sounds echo now, the ohs—
how spontaneous each one was and how exact
in its timing, and in the graded emotion; as if this

is the kind of sound crowds make
at executions of the surely innocent, when even
the expected, the moment of death, must be a shock.

LONDON STREET, WET DAY

I walk fast thinking about time
passing too quickly this week
and wonder how much I've got left
until the pavement—
with its York stone that lights up under rain
to the colour of a shiny dead leaf
the same way it did when I was little,
close enough to it
to enjoy how on some slabs the layers had worn
away in irregular concentric shapes
and on others grey patches had settled like clouds—
the pavement becomes a ladder
and then a rosary
for this habit of thinking about time
which is itself becoming worn
so I look up and further up
blinking at raindrops
and feel sure the trees used to stretch
higher, vertiginously so, against the sky,
even though I was more likely
to find myself
part-way up one then
than now.

LAYERS

It's hot in here after the snow.
                I don't feel it
until we've hung our jackets
                        on chair backs
        unloaded lunch from trays
and sat down. Then I
                        pull my thick jersey off
                                up over my head.
As I push back some
                        flying hair
        I half-see half-sense
your reaction
                a sort of tenderness
        amused and even
                        bemused
which makes me
        aware of myself
                aware that all I want to do is
strip for you
        now
        and press my whole length
                        close against yours.

Did you sense this
                when I turned away
        to fold the jersey?
                        Maybe you did but
it is more beautiful
                not to know.

WAKING UP IN A BASEMENT

Even when I feel the stone weight of the house
and the earth of the hill it's built into
I don't really believe in my death—
not even when I sniff the draught that yesterday
was tainted by the smell of a small animal
decaying in the thistles and tangled grass
under the olive trees whose leaves fall
past the window like elegant rain.
This morning the smell isn't there.
At one time in the past I did, I think,
believe—I certainly lived day after day
in repeatedly unfolding horror.
The sun's come out sideways and is breaking up
orange across the folds of the duvet.
There's a blaze at the corner of my eye
that I need to not look at, partially veiled
though it is by these showers of leaves and
tree-trunks that knot and angle their way skywards.
The bell-tower strikes a half-hour.
The evidence of all the deaths it has tolled
is against me. The dead should crowd
my mind, as do the sweet chestnut and pine trees
that cloak this circular chain of hills.
A pair of shots ring out and the deep valley
moves the noise around: something, perhaps
a deer or wild boar or (heaven forfend) a
small bird may have died now, or be dying—
tasting its own blood amid a sense of
what panic or numb astonishment.

HEART

My heart my heart loyal beast
                    I remember you only if you falter
                    or if I'm sleepless like last night
walker climber diver swimmer
                    when you gave a jolt reminding
                    me that the thought of perpetual
                    motion
fist-sized forge at your every beat
                    contains the terror of its opposite
                    but again today late for a train
                    home I tested you
the red-hot corridors pulsate
                    against gravity leapt off the tube
                    ran up stairs walked up the long
                    escalator stepped
how many deaths how many shocks
                    breathless through ticket gates
                    across the busy hall up again
                    dragged myself up
multi-chambered fortune teller
                    the ramp to the platform and
                    caught my train at the last whistle
how long how long how long

ADAM

Figment may come from the Latin
for imagine, however Anglo-Saxon
the fig sounds, but now figment
of the imagination (surely
a tautology) has merged with
fragment, because a figment has
broken off, a rib of the mind,
and become a person, not that I'd ever
have imagined someone so complete
but if I could, this is how he'd be,
a retrospective fragment
made whole, perfected, my Adam
appearing as if in a dream—
or, more likely, in one.

THE ROSE, THE STARS

I love the early morning when the rose.
Somebody, some time, must have written that.
Hybrid rose, convoluted rose that opens
when no-one else is there, at dawn before
the world sends us away. Whose petals pout:
once my fever made the yellow roses
sneer on a childhood curtain, and afterwards
I couldn't think evil out of the rose.
The rose the morning early when I love.

No rain the longest drought since records first.
Less fruit for my grandmother to bottle,
gleaming on her top larder shelf. Goosegogs,
planets that we topped and tailed—when I knocked
the colander off the step, they spilt to form
a breathing universe, not grass-covered
as Gog and Magog low on her horizon
but the para-greenness of an alien life.
Since first no drought the records' longest rain.

Again last night I met the man of my.
We knew each other long before the world.
A woodpecker drumming has more impact now
on hollow wood than ever love. It's drumming
at spring's front door in winter, Janus bird,
two-headed to stab the year on either side.
Red nape and undertail: for desire, for hope
against the dust and woodworm in its echo.
Of my last night the man I met again.

What knowledge could a spider in the bath.
How many insects has it eaten, to grow
so huge? Web crawler. If anything is what

we think it is, the spider's it, has thread
in all our concerns. Scuttler: multiple legs
remind us of our helplessness. False widow,
rubber spider. Slipping down and climbing
again, alone, stuck in a white expanse.
A bath in knowledge what the spider could.

My head that turns a circle round the sun.
And round inside itself. The jolt when I first,
small child, linked cloud with a shadow falling.
Bag of false coins jangling in a pound shop
already one day nearer death: of this
the sun was the first thing to remind me.
Soon to be shut in night's black box and never
sure of coming back. Though so far, always.
The sun turns round a circle that my head.

Among the stars let's walk forever where.
Where else to go? Their light must be from that time
when we first met. To see it is to see
length beyond length, further than self or any
of our absolutes. A galaxy as thick
with points of light as a beach with glinting sand.
We came from stars: they'll be our ground, for one
moment together before we start to fall.
Let's walk among forever where the stars.

TO THE MOON

1 New Year's Eve

Full moon, casket of wishes, neat-lidded
moon, heavenframed—
ten thousand ghosts are furled inside your circle.

Moon, I will post LOVE, a midnight blue word,
across your face
to roll with you slowly in three dimensions,

turned towards earth and inextricable
from a sky deep
enough to hold all dreams. Looked at for as long

as I look at you, LOVE will soon become
meaningless. So
I will formalise the losing of hope:

for your course, moon, is solitary, you journey
without trading
though not without leading astray. Zone me

into your treeless, pale desolation
O moon, and let
your distance wane my thought by its proportions.

2 *Late February*

O moon, white-gowned eroticist, consumer
of our desires—
look how the world has slowly stripped for you

down to this pre-spring starkness: trees, undergrowth,
blank pavements and
my usual despair, worn out by night after

long dark night of nothing. Not much awake
at this cold hour
except foxes and a few uncurtained

lovers dressed in your steady light. But now,
moon, specialist
in our madness and midnight practices,

now I want to bare all for you, if only
so something must
happen. Reflect me back to myself: rare as

you are, bald as an unearthed Trojan helmet
and as intact,
as necessarily flawed, and silent.

3 *Autumn Equinox*

Moon, pale opposite of a shadow—so
unexpected
at the shore's vanishing point, in balance

with the sun gone down. First inkling: now you
strengthen and rise
full neon, prototype of a mood, over

the sea into violet sky. Your trail runs
faint on blueish
water, but here on the darkening sand

it ripples in salt pools, a long finger
that beckons me.
When I come near, you retreat to a place

beyond understanding, where I can't follow.
Moon, here's a heart
in the sand, and over there a lantern launched

straight for you, a circle of orange flame
soaring towards
destruction: the higher, the more complete.

About the Author

Fiona Moore lives in Greenwich, London. She has an MBA specialising in organisational culture and a degree in Classics. In 2004, she left her Foreign Office career to write. She then worked part-time for Excellent Development, a sustainable development charity specialising in sand dams, and was an assistant editor for *The Rialto* for several years. She is currently a member of the editorial board for *Magma*, reviews poetry (Saboteur Best Reviewer in 2014) and blogs at displacement-poetry. blogspot.co.uk. Her debut pamphlet, *The Only Reason for Time*, was a Guardian poetry book of the year and her second, *Night Letter*, was shortlisted for the Michael Marks Award for Poetry Pamphlets.